GW01458008

Mrs Malone

Book 2

Quercus Poems for Children

Poems chosen by Alan Kerr

Illustrated by Sylvia Mears

ISBN 0-9535684-3-1

Published by Quercus Publications, 8 The Barton,
Bleadon, Weston-super-Mare BS24 0AS

Printed by SP Press, Cheddar, Somerset

Contents

To the Reader

Welcome to "Mrs Malone", a collection of outstanding poems which you are sure to enjoy. Inside you will find some classic favourites such as "Cats", "The Tale of Custard the Dragon" and "Who's Been at the Toothpaste?". You will also discover some less well-known delights including "Cobweb Morning" and "The Donkey".

The anthology contains a mix of poems on a number of themes. Some of the poems are long, some are short; some are serious, some humorous. All of them should be read more than once which will help you get to know them and enjoy them even more.

*When you are reading **look** for the ideas and pictures which the words convey; **listen** for the sounds of the words and their rhymes and rhythms; **feel** the joys and sadnesses, the funny and the serious things; **think about** the thoughts which have been expressed.*

Above all enjoy the pleasure of poetry.

Alan Kerr

Dedicated to the
"Mrs Malones" of this world

Cats

Cats sleep
Anywhere
Any table
Any chair
Top of piano
Window-ledge
In the middle
On the edge
Open drawer
Empty shoe
Anybody's
Lap will do
Fitted in a
Cardboard box
In the cupboard
With your frocks
Anywhere!
They don't care
Cats sleep
Anywhere.

Eleanor Farjeon

Five Eyes

In Hans' old mill his three black cats
Watch his bins for the thieving rats.
Whisker and claw, they crouch in the night,
Their five eyes smouldering green and bright:
Squeaks from the flour sacks, squeaks from where
The cold wind stirs on the empty stair,
Squeaking and scampering, everywhere.
Then down they pounce, now in, now out,
At whisking tail, and sniffing snout;
While lean old Hans he snores away
Till peep of light at break of day;
Then up he climbs to his creaking mill,
Out come his cats all grey with meal -
Jekkel, and Jessup, and one-eyed Jill.

Walter de la Mare

The Donkey

I saw a donkey
  One day old,
His head was too big
  For his neck to hold;
His legs were shaky
  And long and loose,
They rocked and staggered
  And weren't much use.
He tried to gambol
  And frisk a bit,
But he wasn't quite sure
  Of the trick of it.
His queer little coat
  Was soft and grey
And curled at his neck
  In a lovely way.
His face was wistful
  And left no doubt
That he felt life needed
  Some thinking out.
So he blundered round
  In venturous quest,
And then lay flat
  On the ground to rest.
He looked so little
  And weak and slim,
I prayed the world
  Might be good to him.

Gertrude Hinde

The Robin

I tried to write a poem today,
I tried to make it rhyme,
I tried to get the meaning right
But every single time
I thought I'd got the hang of it,
I thought I'd got it right,
I found I couldn't think of a word
To rhyme with bird
Or, that is, robin.

I didn't want to say,
I saw a robin.
It was bobbing
Along and sobbing.
Because it wasn't.

So I started again.

Once, last winter, in the snow,
I was out in the garden
At the bird table,
When I turned round
And saw, on the path beside me,
A robin.

It was so close
I could have touched it.
It took my breath away.

I have never forgotten
The red of it
And the white snow falling.

June Crebbin

The Tale of Custard the Dragon

Belinda lived in a little white house,
With a little black kitten and a little grey mouse,
And a little yellow dog and a little red wagon,
And a realio, trulio, little pet dragon.

Now the name of the little black kitten was Ink,
And the little grey mouse, she called him Blink,
And the little yellow dog was sharp as Mustard,
But the dragon was a coward, and she called him Custard.

Custard the dragon had big sharp teeth,
And spikes on top of him and scales underneath,
Mouth like a fireplace, chimney for a nose,
And realio, trulio daggers on his toes.

Belinda was as brave as a barrel full of bears,
And Ink and Blink chased lions down the stairs,
Mustard was as brave as a tiger in a rage,
But Custard cried for a nice safe cage.

Belinda tickled him, she tickled him unmerciful,
Ink, Blink and Mustard, they rudely called him Percival,
They all sat laughing in the little red wagon
At the realio, trulio, cowardly dragon.

Belinda giggled till she shook the house,
And Blink said Weeck! which is giggling for a mouse,
Ink and Mustard rudely asked his age,
When Custard cried for a nice safe cage.

Suddenly, suddenly they heard a nasty sound,
And Mustard growled, and they all looked around.
Meowch! cried Ink, and Ooh! cried Belinda,
For there was a pirate, climbing in the winda.

Pistol in his left hand, pistol in his right,
And he held in his teeth a cutlass bright,
His beard was black, one leg was wood;
It was clear that the pirate meant no good.

Belinda paled, and she cried Help! Help!
But Mustard fled with a terrified yelp,
Ink trickled down to the bottom of the household,
And little mouse Blink strategically mouseholed.

But up jumped Custard, snorting like an engine,
Clashed his tail like irons in a dungeon,
With a clatter and a clank and a jangling squirm,
He went at the pirate like a robin at a worm.

The pirate gaped at Belinda's dragon,

And gulped some grog from his pocket flagon,

He fired two bullets, but they didn't hit,

And Custard gobbled him, every bit.

        *   *   *   *   *   *

Belinda embraced him, Mustard licked him,

No one mourned for his pirate victim.

Ink and Blink in glee did gyrate

Around the dragon that ate the pirate.

But presently up spoke little dog Mustard,

I'd have been twice as brave if I hadn't been flustered.

And up spoke Ink and up spoke Blink,

We'd have been three times as brave, we think,

And Custard said, I quite agree

That everybody is braver than me.

Belinda still lives in her little white house,

With her little black kitten and her little grey mouse,

And her little yellow dog and her little red wagon,

And her realio, trulio, little pet dragon.

Belinda is as brave as a barrel full of bears,
And Ink and Blink chase lions down the stairs,
Mustard is as brave as a tiger in a rage,
But Custard keeps crying for a nice safe cage.

Ogden Nash

Mrs Malone

Mrs Malone
Lived hard by a wood
All on her lonesome
As nobody should.
With her crust on a plate
And her pot on the coal
And none but herself
To converse with, poor soul.
In a shawl and a hood
She got sticks out-o'-door,
On a bit of old sacking
She slept on the floor,
And nobody, nobody
Asked how she fared
Or knew how she managed,
For nobody cared.
  Why make a pother
  About an old crone?
  What for should they bother
  With Mrs Malone?

One Monday in winter
With snow on the ground
So thick that a footstep
Fell without sound,

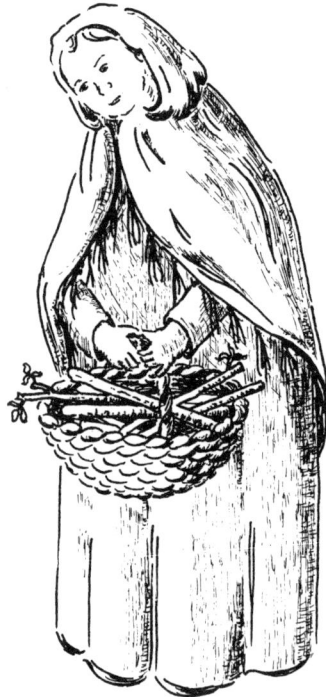

She heard a faint frostbitten
Peck on the pane
And went to the window
To listen again.
There sat a cock-sparrow
Bedraggled and weak,
With half-open eyelid
And ice on his beak.
She threw up the sash
And she took the bird in,
And mumbled and fumbled it
Under her chin.
  "Ye're all of a smother,
  Ye're fair overblown!
  I've room fer another,"
  Said Mrs Malone.

Come Tuesday while eating
Her dry morning slice
With the sparrow a-picking
("Ain't company nice!")
She heard on her doorpost
A curious scratch,
And there was a cat
With its claw on the latch.

It was hungry and thirsty
And thin as a lath,
It mewed and it mowed
On the slithery path.
She threw the door open
And warmed up some pap,
And huddled and cuddled it
In her old lap.
  "There, there, little brother,
  Ye poor skin-an'-bone,
  There's room fer another,"
  Said Mrs Malone.

Come Wednesday while all of them
Crouched on the mat
With a crumb for the sparrow,
A sip for the cat,
There was wailing and whining
Outside in the wood,
And there sat a vixen
With six of her brood.

She was haggard and ragged
And worn to a shred,
And her half-dozen babies
Were only half-fed,
But Mrs Malone, crying
"My! Ain't they sweet!"
Happed them and lapped them
And gave them to eat.
    "You warm yerself, mother,
    Ye're cold as a stone!
    There's room fer another,"
    Said Mrs Malone.

Come Thursday a donkey
Stepped in off the road
With sores on his withers
From bearing a load.
Come Friday when icicles
Pierced the white air
Down from the mountainside
Lumbered a bear.
For each she had something,
If little, to give -
"Lord knows, the poor critters
Must all of 'em live."

She gave them her sacking,
Her hood and her shawl,
Her loaf and her teapot -
She gave them her all.
   "What with one thing and t'other
   Me fambily's grown,
   And there's room fer another,"
   Said Mrs Malone.

Come Saturday evening
When time was to sup
Mrs Malone
Had forgot to sit up.
The cat said *meeow*,
And the sparrow said *peep*,
The vixen, *she's sleeping*,
The bear, *let her sleep*.
On the back of the donkey
They bore her away,
Through trees and up mountains
Beyond night and day,
Till come Sunday morning
They brought her in state
Through the last cloudbank
As far as the Gate.

"Who is it," asked Peter,
"You have with you there?"
And donkey and sparrow,
Cat, vixen and bear
Exclaimed, "Do you tell us
Up here she's unknown?
It's our mother, God bless us!
It's Mrs Malone
Whose havings were few
And whose holding was small
And whose heart was so big
It had room for us all."
Then Mrs Malone
Of a sudden awoke,
She rubbed her two eyeballs
And anxiously spoke:
"Where am I, to goodness,
And what do I see?
My dears, let's turn back,
This ain't no place fer me!"
But Peter said, "Mother
Go in to the Throne.
There's room for another
One, Mrs Malone."

Eleanor Farjeon

Eleanor Farjeon

Eleanor Farjeon was born in London in 1881, the daughter of a popular novelist, Benjamin Farjeon. She had three talented brothers with whom she shared a happy, creative and unconventional childhood. The Farjeon children did not go to school but were educated at home where they were allowed plenty of freedom to play imaginatively but were also encouraged to read a lot. Eleanor's father had thousands of books and it was his custom every Sunday after lunch to give each child a book to keep and read.

Eleanor loved reading and from an early age began to write: stories, poems, playlets and rhymes. Supported in her writing by her father she would slide her offerings under his study door and run back to her room to wait for his comments on what she had written. When she was seven she could already type and correct proofs.

In 1903 her father died and it took Eleanor a long time to recover from the shock. She escaped into her writing, and her stories, articles and poems began to be published successfully. Although some of her writing was for adults it is for her stories and poems for children that she is best known. Her poems, with their varied subject matter and flowing rhythm, sparkle as much today as when they were first written.

As she grew older Eleanor was known as a jolly person, full of fun with a warm smile and twinkling eyes. She was a friend to many people and particularly enjoyed the company of children and cats. Her memorable poem about the sleeping habits of her four-footed friends is a favourite with everyone.

1881 – 1965

Two Limericks

There was an Old Man with a beard,
Who said: "It is just as I feared! –
Two Owls and a Hen,
Four Larks and a Wren,
Have all built their nests in my beard!"

There was an Old Man of The Hague,
Whose ideas were excessively vague;
He built a balloon
To examine the moon,
That deluded Old Man of The Hague.

Edward Lear

Who's Been at the Toothpaste?

Who's been at the toothpaste?
I know some of you do it right
and you squeeze the tube from the bottom
and you roll up the tube as it gets used up, don't
you?

But somebody
somebody here -
you know who you are
you dig your thumb in
anywhere, anyhow
and you've turned that tube of toothpaste
into a squashed sock.
You've made it so hard to use
it's like trying to get toothpaste
out of a packet of nuts.

You know who you are.
I won't ask you to come out here now
but you know who you are.

And then you went and left the top off didn't you?
So the toothpaste turned to cement.

People who do things like that should . . .
you should be ashamed of yourself.

I am.

Michael Rosen

UR 2 GOOD

```
UR   2    GOOD
     2    ME
     2    BE
     4    GOT
   ----
    10
```

Michael Rosen

I'm Just Going Out for a Moment

I'm just going out for a moment.
Why?
To make a cup of tea.
Why?
Because I'm thirsty.
Why?
Because it's hot.
Why?
Because the sun's shining.
Why?
Because it's summer.
Why?
Because that's when it is.
Why?
Why don't you stop saying why?
Why?
Tea-time. That's why.
High-time-you-stopped-saying-why-time.

What?

Michael Rosen

Michael Rosen

Michael Rosen was born in the London Borough of Harrow in 1946. He completed his formal education by studying English at Oxford University.

His first book of poems for children was called "Mind Your Own Business", and it contained poems which were very different in content and style from those which had been written before.

Using his own memories of childhood and observations of his own children a stream of situations with which children and adults can identify flows through his poetry with realism, humour and sensitivity.

His "Eddie" poems have delighted readers of all ages with their amusing and loving tales about the young toddler. "Eddie and the Nappy", "Eddie and the Birthday" and "Eddie and the Shreddies" are three of these memorable poems which can be found in "Quick, Let's Get Out of Here".

Where Go the Boats?

Dark brown is the river,
Golden is the sand.
It flows along for ever,
With trees on either hand.

Green leaves a-floating,
Castles of the foam,
Boats of mine a-boating –
Where will all come home?

On goes the river
And out past the mill,
Away down the valley,
Away down the hill.

Away down the river,
A hundred miles or more,
Other little children
Shall bring my boats ashore.

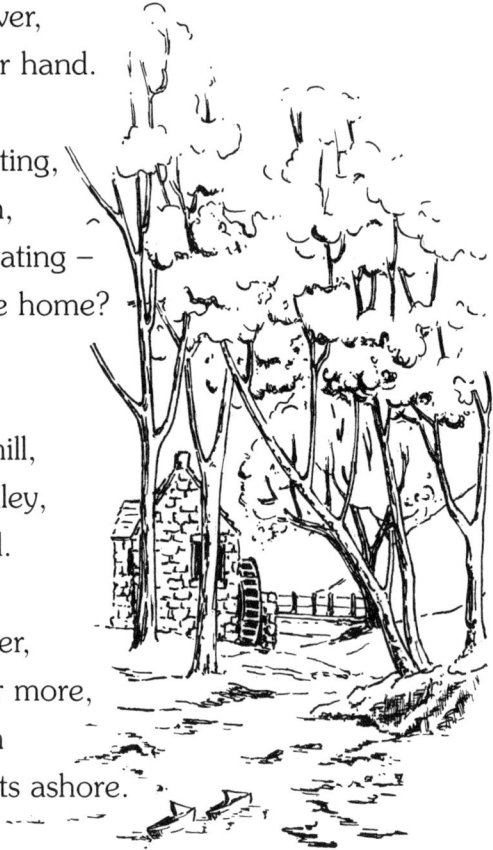

Robert Louis Stevenson

The Land of Counterpane

When I was sick and lay a-bed,
I had two pillows at my head,
And all my toys beside me lay
To keep me happy all the day.

And sometimes for an hour or so
I watched my leaden soldiers go,
With different uniforms and drills,
Among the bed-clothes, through the hills;

And sometimes sent my ships in fleets
All up and down among the sheets;
Or brought my trees and houses out,
And planted cities all about.

I was the giant great and still
That sits upon the pillow-hill,
And sees before him, dale and plain,
The pleasant land of counterpane.

Robert Louis Stevenson

Robert Louis Stevenson

Born in Edinburgh in 1850 Robert Louis Stevenson became one of the great writers of the nineteenth century. He wrote novels, plays, poems, essays and travel books. Many of his books are still read and enjoyed today and have become classics. They include "Treasure Island", "Kidnapped" and "The Strange Case of Dr Jekyll and Mr Hyde".

As an only child he was largely brought up by his beloved nurse "Cummy". His childhood was greatly affected by his poor health and he spent many wakeful, feverish nights being soothed by his father telling him stories and by Cummy singing hymns and psalms to him. He often had terrifying nightmares. Two of his favourite toys were his lead soldiers and cardboard theatres and he spent hours creating imaginary adventures with them.

His father hoped that Louis, as he was often known, would become a lighthouse engineer like himself but although he studied engineering at university he decided to become a writer.

Throughout his life he relished the challenge of travelling and on one occasion he hiked through some wild hill country in France with a donkey as his only companion. Eventually, accompanied by his family, he went to live on the island of Samoa thousands of miles away from Scotland. There he continued to write but did not find the happiness he had been seeking. He died shortly after his forty-fourth birthday.

Robert Louis Stevenson's poems for children, "A Child's Garden of Verses", were written over a number of years. They vividly recapture the joys and imaginings of childhood - the childhood of today, yesterday and, hopefully, tomorrow.

1850 – 1894

Pocket

In my pocket were -

Two broken biscuits
Three torn tissues
Four cracking conkers
Five smooth stones
Six sticky sweets
Seven stamps for swops
Eight copper coins
Nine coloured crayons
Ten matching marbles

and

one

HUGE

hole!

June Crebbin

In the Playground

In the playground
Some run round
Chasing a ball
Or chasing each other;
Some pretend to be
Someone on TV;
Some walk
And talk,
Some stand
On their hands
Against the wall
And some do nothing at all.

Stanley Cook

Matilda Runs Away

Matilda Alice Tomkinson
This little story is about;
She said she'd run away from home
Because they told her not to shout.
She ran along the garden path,
And through the gate, and down the lane,
And then, as no one followed her,
She turned – and ran back home again.

She saw her father in the hall,
And so she gave the door a slam,
And shouted from the garden path,
"I'm going to run away, I am."
Then turned and ran away once more,
Out through the gate, and down the lane.
But no one seemed to notice it –
And so she ran back home again.

Her Auntie, in the drawing-room,
Was sitting pouring out the tea.
Matilda looked at her and said,
"I'm going to run away, you see."
Then turned and quickly ran outside,
And through the gate, and down the lane.
But no one called to her, "Don't go."
And so she ran back home again.

Matilda found her brother Phil,
And said, "I'm going to run away."
But Phil said, "What again, you goat?"
And took his bat and went to play.
Matilda clattered down the stairs,
And sang as she went down the lane.
But no one seemed to hear, nor care,
And so she ran back home again.

Matilda sat upon the step,
And tried to think the matter out.
And presently her mother came,
And said, "Dear – what's it all about?"
And when her mother heard the tale,
She said, "Let's see what we can do.
Now I'll come with you to the gate,
And stand and wave goodbye to you."

Matilda started off once more,
But turned, when halfway down the lane,
And saw her mother's arms outstretched –
And so she ran back home again.

Marion St John Webb

Autumn

Whirling leaves, golden and brown,
Twisting and turning,
Hurrying down.

Driving wind, gusty and strong,
Whistling and sighing,
Rushing along.

Scudding clouds, grey-leaden sky,
Laughing and playing,
Galloping by.

Roaming birds, gathered for flight,
Chirping and preening,
Seeking sunlight.

Curling smoke, mindful of fires,
Blowing and puffing,
Hiding the spires.

Drooping rose, scatter to earth,
Dying and fading,
Waiting new birth.

F Politzer

Autumn

Yellow the bracken,
Golden the sheaves,
Rosy the apples,
Crimson the leaves;
Mist on the hillside,
Clouds grey and white.
Autumn good morning!
Summer, good night!

Florence Hoatson

Cobweb Morning

On a Monday morning
We do spellings and Maths.
And silent reading.

But on the Monday
After the frost
We went straight outside.

Cobwebs hung in the cold air,
Everywhere.
All around the playground,
They clothed the trees,
Dressed every bush
In veils of fine white lace.

Each web,
A wheel of patient spinning.
Each spider,
Hidden,
Waiting.

Inside,
We worked all morning
To capture the outside.

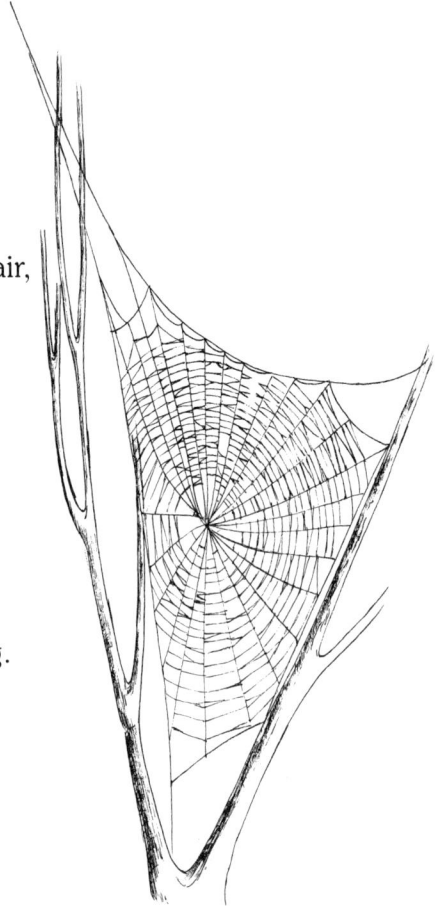

Now
In our patterns and poems
We remember
The cobweb morning.

June Crebbin

June Crebbin

In her work as a primary school teacher June Crebbin found inspiration for many of the poems in her collection called "The Jungle Sale".

She has every poet's great gift of taking a thought, an idea or an image and lovingly crafting it in words to present a vivid picture to the reader. This makes her poems a pleasure to read the first time and makes you want to read them again and again.

Beneath her clear, everyday language, with its humour and gentle style, lie all sorts of interesting thoughts and observations – especially about children and school!

For Them

Before you bid, for Christmas' sake,
   Your guests to sit at meat,
Oh please to save a little cake
   For them that have no treat.

Before you go down party-dressed
   In silver gown or gold,
Oh please to send a little vest
   To them that still go cold.

Before you give your girl and boy
   Gay gifts to be undone,
Oh please to spare a little toy
   To them that will have none.

Before you gather round the tree
   To dance the day about,
Oh please to give a little glee
   To them that go without.

Eleanor Farjeon

Acknowledgements

Grateful thanks are due to the following for permission to use copyright material:

David Higham Associates for **Cats** by Eleanor Farjeon from *The Children's Bells,* Oxford University Press; for **Mrs Malone** and **For Them** by Eleanor Farjeon from *Silver Sand and Snow,* Michael Joseph; June Crebbin for her poems **The Robin, Pocket** and **Cobweb Morning** from *The Jungle Sale,* Viking Kestrel 1988; the Literary Trustees of Walter de la Mare, and the Society of Authors as their representative, for **Five Eyes** by Walter de la Mare; Andre Deutsch Limited for **The Tale of Custard the Dragon** by Ogden Nash from *I Wouldn't Have Missed It,* 1936; Penguin Books Limited for **Who's Been at the Toothpaste?** by Michael Rosen from *You Tell Me* by Roger McGough and Michael Rosen, Kestrel 1979 © Michael Rosen 1979; PFD for **UR 2 GOOD** by Michael Rosen; Scholastic Limited for **I'm Just Going Out for a Moment** by Michael Rosen from *Wouldn't You Like to Know?*; Mrs S Matthews for **In the Playground** by Stanley Cook, © the estate of Stanley Cook, first published in *Wordhouses* by the author and then in *A Second Poetry Book,* Oxford University Press, ed John Foster; Oxford University Press for **Autumn** by F Politzer from *Wordscapes,* Barry Maybury, Oxford University Press, 1970.